Valerie Bloom was born in Jamaica and came to England in 1979. She studied English, African and Caribbean literature and history at the University of Kent and was awarded an Honorary Masters degree from the university in 1995. Valerie has conducted lots of writing and performance workshops in schools and colleges and has performed widely in Britain and the Caribbean. Her poems have been included in over two hundred anthologies and in the National Curriculum and have appeared in *Poems on the Underground* and as the *Independent* newspaper's Poem of the Day. *One River, Many Creeks*, *Whoop an' Shout* and *Surprising Joy*, Valerie's first novel, are also published by Macmillan.

Jane Eccles has finally escaped from London and is happily settling into the rural life in Hampshire with her husband, Graham, and son, Theo. All that's missing is a dog . . .

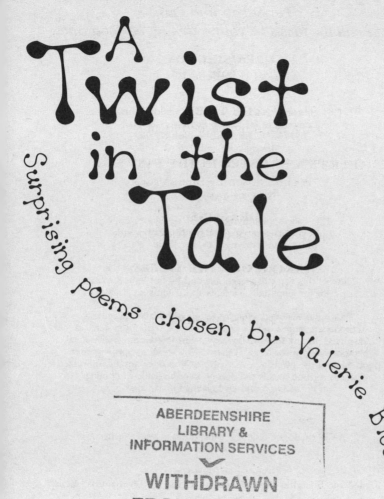

A Twist in the Tale

Surprising poems chosen by Valerie Bloom

MACMILLAN CHILDREN'S BOOKS

For Sarah and Dan.
May all the twists in your journeys be good ones.

First published 2005 by Macmillan Children's Books
a division of Macmillan Publishers Limited
20 New Wharf Road, London N1 9RR
Basingstoke and Oxford
Associated companies throughout the world
www.panmacmillan.com

ISBN 978-0-330-39899-2

3 5 7 9 8 6 4

A CIP catalogue record for this book is available from
the British Library.

Typeset by Nigel Hazle
Printed and bound in Great Britain by Mackays of Chatham plc, Kent

Contents

Guess What I'm Painting

Guess what I'm painting.
Don't dare say it's a mess!
What do you think it's meant to be?
Go on, guess.

No, it's not an earwig . . .
Nor a vampire bat . . .
It's not an oak tree either.
How could you think that?

It's not a caterpillar . . .
Nor a kangaroo.
You're a really rotten guesser:
It's obvious – it's you!

Eric Finney

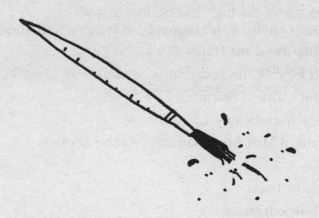

The Thing

Something crept in with the moon last night
A thing
This new thing in our house
And it wasn't a cat and it wasn't a dog
And it certainly wasn't a mouse
This thing
No it certainly wasn't a mouse.

It must be an alien, I thought to myself
This thing
Yes an alien, that's what it must be
That flew through the dark in a silver ship
At midnight silently
This thing
By starlight secretly.

I could tell it was trying to speak to me
This thing
To speak through the bedroom wall
But it spoke in a language of gurgles and shouts
That made no sense at all
This thing
No it made no sense at all.

I had to find out what it looked like
This thing
This thing in Mum's room next door
So I crept down the hallway and into her room
And there by her side I saw
This thing
This thing is what I saw.

'Oh, Mum,' I said, 'what is it
That thing
With its face all wrinkled and red?'
And she smiled and placed its fist in mine.
'Meet your new little sister,' she said
She said
'Meet your lovely new sister,' she said.

Gareth Owen

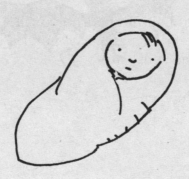

Batty

The baby bat

Screamed out in fright,

'Turn on the dark,

I'm afraid of the light.'

Shel Silverstein

4

Look Out!

The witches mumble horrid chants,
You're scolded by five thousand aunts,
  A Martian pulls a fearsome face
  And hurls you into Outer Space,
You're tied in front of whistling trains,
A tomahawk has sliced your brains,
  The tigers snarl, the giants roar,
  You're sat on by a dinosaur.
In vain you're shouting 'Help' and 'Stop',
The walls are spinning like a top,
  The earth is melting in the sun
  And all the horror's just begun.
And, oh, the screams, the thumping hearts
That awful night before school starts.

Max Fatchen

The New Kid on the Block

There's a new kid on the block,
and boy, that kid is tough,
that new kid punches hard,
that new kid plays real tough,
that new kid's big and strong,
with muscles everywhere,
that new kid tweaked my arm,
that new kid pulled my hair.

The new kid likes to fight,
and picks on all the guys,
that new kid scares me some
(that new kid's twice my size),
that new kid stomped my toes,
that new kid swiped my ball,
that new kid's really bad,
I don't care for her at all.

Jack Prelutsky

Dad, the Amateur Hypnotist

Follow my
swinging watch
with your
eyes. Now
you are
feeling sleepy . . .
When I
count to
three and
click my
fingers, you
will wake
up, then
bark like
a dog.
One. Two.
Three.

Click!
'Miaow.'

Mike Johnson

The Three Wise Women

When the three wise men
left by camel, they
left three wise women.

One said: 'He took gold
for baby Jesus –
now just one hour old!'

'Mine took frankincense,'
said the second. 'Men
have no common sense!'

'And my man took myrrh
so the baby smells
doubly sweet – yes, sir!'

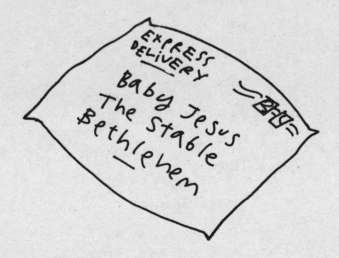

8

Being worldly wise,
the wives made tiny
nappies to his size —

gifts he needed most —
and packaged them to
send by express post.

Debjani Chatterjee

The Terror

You might not believe my story
About my brother, Lew.
It's really rather shocking
But I promise it's all true.
Lew's always been a terror,
His behaviour is quite wild,
'I've never,' his poor teacher wailed,
'Met such a naughty child.
He's put worms into the sand pit,
Cut off Natasha's hair,
He stamps, he shouts, he kicks, he spits
And drives me to despair.'
'Lew's just like that at home as well!'
My parents both agreed.
'We've tried our best to calm him
Yet we, frankly, don't succeed.'
Lew's seen six different doctors,
A child psychologist too,
Who, when my brother bit her, cried:
'There's nothing I can do.'
And none of us could understand
Why Lew was so disturbed
Until, one night, four months ago,
When something weird occurred.
The night was wild and stormy,
I was woken by the roar
Of thunder and the howling wind
Rattling at the door.
Standing by the window, I saw
The full moon's beam,

Then, as the clouds passed over it,
I heard my brother scream.
An agonizing, piercing sound,
Which gave me such a fright.
I burst into his bedroom,
Switching on the light.
And I'll not forget the horror
Of seeing, on his bed,
A furry, sharp-fanged creature
With mad eyes, glistening red.
The ears were growing longer and
Fingers turned to claws,
Its nose grew black and shiny,
I didn't know the cause . . .
But my brother, Lew, was changing
To a werewolf, fierce and hairy,
Growling, getting set to pounce,
I'll tell you, it was scary!

'Nice Wolfie, Wolfie, please don't bite . . .
SIT! That's a good boy . . . good.'
And do you know, he sat quite still;
I never thought he would!
Trembling, I edged closer,
Fighting back my fear,
'Down boy, that's right, down,'
I said, as I drew near.
His top lip curled, his teeth blazed white,
His tongue shot out so quick,
With a slurping, splashy, sloppy squelch,
He gave my face a lick!
'Stop that now,' I said. 'It tickles!
I know, let's play a game.'
So we played 'fetch the ball' all night.
Our Wolfie was quite tame.
My parents woke, they came to look,
Yet couldn't believe their eyes.
I was playing with a werewolf,
My brother, in disguise!
He let them rub behind his ears,
'Good boy,' they said. 'Good lad.'
The transformation, we agreed,
Wasn't all that bad.
But when the sun replaced the moon
My brother reappeared.
'Hey, what yer doin' in my room?
Get lost,' my brother sneered.
He threw his slippers at my dad,
Then, just to make it plain,
Lew hit my mum and kicked my shin,
He really is a pain!

So now, you'll maybe understand
Why we all look forward to
The time of month when the moon is full,
And the wolf replaces Lew.
It's a time of celebration
A nice, relaxing treat.
Cos as a boy my brother's awful, but . . .
As a wolf he's really sweet.

Sandra Glover

Learning to Swim

Teacher said it was easy,
      learning to swim.
Put a smile on your face,
      no need to look grim.
Just stand on the bank,
      full of trust and belief,
Then plunge, like a dart,
      to the water beneath.

Heart pounding, I stood,
      doing what I was told.
I stood there for ages,
      all shaking and cold.
Goose pimples growing,
      legs turning to jelly,
I leaped like a salmon –
      and flopped on my belly.

Lashing the water,
      trying not to be beat,
I finally managed
      to stand on my feet.
Thankfully knowing
      I was over the worst,
I was feeling quite glad
      that I'd said I'd go first.

I thought of my classmates
    all waiting their turn,
And how Teacher fibbed about
    'easy to learn'.
I crawled from the water
    and grinned through my pain,
And Teacher said,
    'Super! Please show us again!'

Brian G. D'Arcy

A Story of Snowballs

Only last week down by the canal
I met Shiner Smith, my very best pal
A cold winter's day filled up with snow
The water was grey, the going was slow.

We both felt so bored, there was nothing to do
But then a small pleasure craft chugged into view
A big man with a beard was steering the boat
Wrapped up in a scarf and thick overcoat.

Shiner looked hard at this nautical bloke
Said, 'Let's chuck a snowball, just for a joke.'
'You what?' I replied. 'You wouldn't dare.'
But one had already whizzed through the air!

So I scraped up some snow hard in my fist
The boat hardly moved, it couldn't be missed
I gave my packed snowball one final squeeze
Then shouted, 'Oi, Fatty, have one of these!'

He was so angry, red-faced and sore
He felt even worse when we threw twenty more
He shouted, 'Hey stop that. Just pack it in!'
And Shiner got him, smack on the chin.

I landed a beauty right down his neck
Another one burst like a bomb on the deck
He slipped on the bits, lost his footing and fell
Bounced like a ball and gave a loud yell.

We lobbed him some others, ran from the path
Into the woods and had a good laugh
Then we said goodbye and soon forgot
About our sad sailor and the soaking he'd got.

Several days later school started again
I was feeling OK, so was Shiner, but when
We walked through the gate and over the yard
We noticed our teacher glaring quite hard.

Beside him there stood a man that we knew
Last time we'd seen him he'd turned the air blue
Shouting and yelling through a big beard
I started to feel all shaky and weird

He snarled, 'Glad to meet you. Just couldn't wait
I'm your new head teacher, I'm Mr Tate.
So you like to snowball?' he said with a sneer.
'Well, I'd like to have a word in your ear.'

'I hope you enjoyed your moment of fun
I've just phoned your parents to say what you've done
But this time my friends it's my turn to win.
In fact here they are! Come in! Let's begin!'

David Harmer

17

Moaning Minnie

'You could moan for England,'
is what Mum said to me.
When asked for his opinion
Dad said, 'I agree.'

He entered me in a regional heat
and I easily got through
but by the time I reached the final
I said, 'Uh! Do I have to?'

They pushed me on to the platform
and gave me a microphone
so I took a breath as deep as the sea
and then began to moan.

I moaned about the weather.
I moaned about TV.
I moaned about my brother.
I moaned about being me.

I moaned about the whole wide world.
I moaned about our sofa.
I planned to moan for hours
but they said, 'STOP! It's over.'

'That's it. You're the winner.
Now what have you got to say?'
'Me? A winner! Wow!
You've really made my day.'

'Sorry,' they said, 'trick question.
A ruse. A crafty test.
You would have kept on moaning
if you really were the best.'

Bernard Young

Invisible Boy

Invisibility potions
take time to prepare.
When he looked in his mirror . . .
'Yes! I'm not there.'

He pulled off his pyjamas,
'Now my fun can begin.'
Ran straight to his school
in invisible skin.

Once in the playground,
tripped up his worst enemy;
knocked a drink from the hand
of 'teacher's pet' Naomi.

A bully he hated
got shoved hard, in the back.
Our invisible hero threw
balls – landed 'Thwack!'

At this time (with no clothes on),
he'd grown colder and colder,
but this merely made his plans
bolder and bolder.

Marched into assembly,
stood beside the headmaster
(so thin is that line
between triumph and disaster).

The head, with composure,
gave one polite cough.
Invisibility potions
can quickly wear off.

Mike Johnson

Sir Donald Dimplechin

In the days of tall tales and short dragons
Lived a knight called Sir Don Dimplechin
Who longed to join Arthur's Round Table
But was told that his chances were slim.

His wardrobe was full of flash armour
His jaw was as strong as his sword
He fancied himself a real charmer
Yet he felt overlooked and ignored.

The king never asked him to battles
As a knight he'd been left on the shelf
He needed a deed that was daring
To help make a name for himself.

So he sent out his put-upon pageboy
With instructions to search far and wide
For a damsel to save, to make him look brave
And if poss. double up as his bride.

So his servant set off through the forest
And travelled for mile after mile
Till one day as he passed through a clearing
He spied what would make his boss smile.

On a hill, a dark sinister tower
Stood encircled by brambles and broom
With no windows save right at the summit
Where a damsel paced round a round room.

22

All alone in her circular chamber
She gazed from each window in turn
He watched as she scanned the horizon
Her face full of earnest concern.

But as the boy stood there fixated
He was roused from his deep reverie
By the sight of a craggy-faced creature
Creeping out from the dense shrubbery.

'Twas a man caped in black like a raven
Dark eyes peered from under his hood
And though wizened and small he was able to
　haul
A big cart full of timber and wood.

The page asked his name and his business
He looked up and croaked, 'Old Magee.
I been an' chopped down tower staircase
And now I got firewood for free!'

With that the old man gave a cackle
And scurried away out of sight
So the servant ran home to his master
And told of the poor damsel's plight.

Sir Don decreed, 'Quick, build a ladder
For I dread to imagine the worst
If we leave the maid there much longer
Some other will rescue her first.'

The poor page would soon regret making
A ladder so tall and so strong
For as they trudged back to the clearing
Don left him to drag it along.

They arrived and Don slashed through the thicket
Till he stopped and said, 'Hang on a mo.
You boy, go ahead, check those nettles are dead
There are chinks in this armour, you know.'

They at last reached the foot of the tower
Don straightened his chain mail and tie
He called, 'Can you hear me, sweet maiden?'
But was baffled to hear her reply.

She shouted down, 'Do you need saving?'
He yelled up, 'I thought it was you!'
She cried, 'You stay there, I can't hear you from 'ere
I'll come down and see what I can do.'

The girl disappeared from the window
And before he could talk to her more
'Twas a whoosh and a 'Wheeeee!' and a turn of a key
And the damsel appeared at the door.

Don Dimplechin looked quite astonished
The maiden just stood there amused
As she watched the knight pout as he tried to work out
How his mission had got so confused.

24

He said, 'How'd you get here so quickly
Without the stairs Old Magee stole?'
She explained, 'I'm the new firefighter
And this is me fireman's pole.'

The damsel called after Sir Donald
As he stormed off all sulky and vexed,
'If you see Old Magee could you tell him
I'm wanting the garden done next.'

Louise Thomas

Football in the Rain

It's drizzling.
'Football practice!'
'Oh, sir!
Do we have to?'
We look hopefully at Mr Tompkins,
But he says,
'Don't be such babies!'
So out we go.

It's raining harder.
We all start to moan,
'Can't we go in, sir?
We're getting soaked!'
But Mr Tompkins is not impressed.
'Tough. Get on with it!'
He says, putting up his umbrella
And retreating to the touchline.

It's coming down in buckets.
There are puddles all over the pitch
And the rest is just mud.
Eddy falls over
And comes up looking like
The Mud Monster from Hell.
We all start falling over,
Because we all want to look like that.

26

It's really chucking it down.
Mr Tompkins gets rain in his whistle.
Gurgle-gurgle-PHEEEP!
'Everybody in!'
We start moaning again.
'Oh, sir!
Do we have to?'

David Orme

27

Rattlesnake Meat

A gourmet challenged me to eat
A tiny bit of rattlesnake meat,
Remarking, 'Don't look horror-stricken,
You'll find it tastes a lot like chicken.'
It did.
Now chicken I cannot eat
Because it tastes like rattlesnake meat.

Ogden Nash

28

Cinderella's Revenge

They called me Cinderella
Cos I slept beside the cinders.
My sisters kept on shouting
And my life was dark despair.
But then there was some business
With a fairy and a pumpkin
And a rather pretty slipper
Which I left upon the stair.
So now I am a princess
And I'm living in a castle.
The prince is very charming
And I get a lot to spend.

As for my two sisters –
Well, they're squatting in a hovel.
And do I care a single jot?
No, I do not. The End.

Kaye Umansky

Cindy Reller

Cindy Reller
Read the News,
'Royal Disco,
Rock & Blues.'
Knew her clothes were
Far too scruffy
(Cleaning jobs don't
Pay enuffy).

Boris Buttons
(Kind but poor)
Helped her brush the
Cafe floor.
'Cheer up, Cindy,
There's a chance
You may still go
To the dance.
My last pound could
Set you free
If you try the
Lottery.'

On the TV
Screen that night
Cindy's numbers
Sparkled bright.
Up she jumped from
Battered chair,
'I've become a
Millionaire!'
Sold her story
To the press,
Bought a cool
Designer dress,
Crossed the town to
Meet her Prince
Wearing shoes that
Made her wince . . .

. . . Kicked the shiny
Things away,
Danced barefoot till
Break of day,
While the Prince
Turned up his nose
At the sight of
Cindy's toes.
Chose instead her
Ugly sister
(A girl prepared to
Risk a blister).

Meanwhile, Cindy
Didn't care –
Bought the cafe
In the square,
Changed its name to
'Dream Come True'

AND MARRIED BUTTONS!
(Quite right too.)

Clare Bevan

Snake in School

One year in the monsoon season
We all screamed – and with good reason –
A water snake had come to school!
But Mister Singh just kept his cool.
He chased him out of our school gate
And told him off for being late!

Debjani Chatterjee

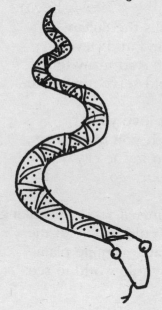

A Final Appointment

Enter the servant Abdul
His face ashy grey,
Fear in his eyes –
He has seen Death today.

Begs release of his master,
Plans instant flight:
'I must be far from
This city tonight!'

'Why?' asks the Sultan,
A man kind and clever.
'You have said many times
You would serve me forever.'

'Master, I love you,
That much you must know,
But down in the city
A half hour ago

'Death himself was out walking,
Reached cold hands for me:
The threat was quite plain
For the whole world to see.

'I must leave Death behind!
To Baghdad I'll take flight.
Master, give me a horse –
I can be there tonight!'

So Abdul escapes
Fear driving him on,
And very soon after
His servant has gone

The Sultan himself
Walks out in the city,
Walks among cripples
And beggars with pity;

Like Abdul, meets Death
As he walks in that place,
Peers into the folds of his cloak
For his face;

Sees it not; hears a voice
That is cold, clear and dry:
'Look not for my face –
See that and you die.'

But the Sultan speaks boldly
Asking Death, 'For what cause
Did you threaten this morning
To make Abdul yours?'

Death replied, 'To your servant
I issued no threat.
Indeed, sir, I knew that
His time was not yet.

'This morning your servant
Had nothing to fear;
He was taken aback
To see the man here;

'Gave me a start of surprise,
Knowing well that I had
An appointment with Abdul
Tonight in Baghdad.'

Eric Finney

Intelligence Test

'What do you use your eyes for?'
The white-coated man enquired.
'I use my eyes for looking,'
Said Toby, '– unless I'm tired.'

'I see. And then you close them,'
Observed the white-coated man.
'Well done. A very good answer.
Let's try another one.

'What is your nose designed for?
What use is the thing to you?'
'I use my nose for smelling,'
Said Toby, 'don't you, too?'

'I do indeed,' said the expert.
'That's what the thing is for.
Now I've another question to ask you,
Then there won't be any more.

'What are your ears intended for?
Those things at each side of your head?
Come on – don't be shy – I'm sure you can say.'
'For washing behind,' Toby said.

Vernon Scannell

Second Language

Mama Cat sat
in her basket
with her kittens.
She washed them,
shlurrrp, shlurrrp, shlurrrp,
and she purred,
prrrrrr, prrrrrr, prrrrrr.
The kittens clambered
over each other to get under
her tongue
and they purred,
prrrrrr, prrrrrr, prrrrrr.

But outside the door was the dog.
Snerrrf, snerrrf, snerrrf:
he could smell the cats.
He scrabbled and scrooged at the carpet,
he tried to burrow under the door,
he jumped up at the handle,
BANG, BANG, BANG
against the door.
He caught the handle
with his paw,
it went down,
the latch went in,
the door opened,
the dog ran into the room,
up to the basket.
Eyes wide, ears forward, tail wagging, the dog barked,
Grrrrufff! Grrrrufff! Grrrrufff!

Grrrrufff
grrrrufff
grrrrufff!

Mama Cat rose up
on to her toes,
her kittens cowered at her feet.
Her back arched in a hoop,
her tail fluffed out like a bottlebrush,
her ears flat against her head.
She opened her mouth and . . .
she barked,
Grrrrufff! Grrrrufff! Grrrrufff!

The dog jumped back in surprise.
His ears went down,
his tail drooped,
he howled in fear,
Owwwwwwww! Owwwwwwww! Owwwwwwww!
He turned and ran
out of the room,
down the hall,
out of the front door,
down the path,
out of the gate,
down the street
and was never seen again.

Mama Cat sank back
down in the basket.
Her fur flattened,
her tail went down,
her ears went forward.
She returned to washing her kittens,
shlurrrp, shlurrrp, shlurrrp,
and she purred,
prrrrrr, prrrrrr, prrrrrr.

One of her kittens put
his head on one side and said,
'Wow, Mama, I never knew you could do that!'
Mama Cat stopped washing
and said,
'Well mind you remember it, so that in future
you'll listen when I tell you how useful it is
to have a second language.'

Pamela Marre

The Crunch

The lion and his tamer
They had a little tiff,
For the lion limped too lamely –
The bars had bored him stiff.

No call to crack your whip, sir!
Said the lion then irate:
No need to snap my head off,
Said the tamer – but too late.

Gerda Mayer

Frog Prince

I don't know why I kissed the frog,
Frogs aren't really my thing –
Nor is slime, but anyway I did.
And then there was this mad explosion –
A sudden whoosh within the empty air
Then the space set solid with long folded legs,
Arms, and a crouching body
Quite unused to standing up.

It seems he was a prince,
Cursed to frogliness by some passing witch.
He'd spent years in that pond
And now he wept for all the little tadpoles
That he'd left behind,
For family life lived under water,
For algae and for spirogyra weed.
His body may have sprung back to a man's,
But underneath his new pink skin
A frog's heart beat, a frog's green soul
Breathed in his breast.

I pitied him
And kissed him once again –
Reversed the uncursing of the curse,
Returned him to his former slimy state.
All should have ended well.
I meant to mend his broken froggy heart,
Meant to soothe him and placate him.
Sadly at that very moment
A heron came and ate him.

Jan Dean

If

If only my head wasn't heavy as lead
And that glow didn't come from this floor,
If I wasn't so nervy, my mind topsy-turvy
And there wasn't a shadow on the door,
If my ears didn't hear and my eyes didn't stare at
Things no one else hears or sees,
If the dogs didn't bark, if outside wasn't dark
And I didn't have the shakes in my knees,
If I wasn't so sure that that ear-splitting snore
Couldn't have come from anyone who's alive,
If my heart didn't leap, if my 'flesh' didn't creep
And I was certain this night I'd survive,
If this night weren't so long, if that low mournful song
Didn't freeze every thought in my brain,
If I could be assured that the scuttling I heard
Was only the rats in the drain,
If that shape that I see was the branch of a tree
A shadow cast by the cloud-shrouded moon,
If I could understand why it looks like a hand
Conducting some unearthly tune,
If all that I've said were just in my head
And that whole thing wasn't so daunting,
I could return to my grave feeling ever so brave
And quite satisfied with my first haunting.

Valerie Bloom

Postcard from Lilliput

Much news but
little space
on Lilliput
cards, so use
imagination.
Gulliver

Debjani Chatterjee

45

The Tale of the Ugly Duckling

Beside a river, in some reeds,
  a duck sat on her nest.
She laid six eggs and kept them warm
  tucked close beneath her breast.

Day in, day out, she guarded them,
  but mothers need to feed.
So every now and then she'd leave
  the eggs and dive for weed.

One day, returning to her nest,
  she blinked, and quacked, 'Great Heaven!
I could have sworn six eggs were here,
  but now I find there's seven!'

Just then, the eggs began to crack
  and tiny creatures hatch.
Six little ducklings, all the same
  . . . and one that didn't match.

Six little fluffy yellow chicks,
  and one with not one feather.
In fact, quite bald, with skin that looked
  a lot like lumpy leather.

He quickly knew that he was odd
  so hid himself away.
He watched the other ducklings swim
  and duck and dive and play.

And as he peered out through the reeds
  and saw the lively brood,
his thoughts were not of family love.
  Oh no, they were of . . . food!

He waddled out on to the bank
  and murmured with a smile,
'An ugly duckling I am not.
  I am a CROCODILE!'

Marianne Chipperfield

Beauty-Sleeping

The young prince was handsome,
    Dashing and bold.
His armour was silver,
    His hair gleamed like gold.

He galloped about –
    As a handsome prince should –
Berating the baddies,
    Assisting the good.

Then he came to a garden
    So thorny and thick
He could hardly get in there.
    He found a big stick.

Beat his way to the door,
    Then forced his way through.
The stairs rose before him
    And up them he flew.

He discovered a chamber,
    A dull, dusty room,
Where an army of spiders
    Wove webs in the gloom.

A beautiful princess
         Lay sleeping inside.
He unbuckled his armour
         And rushed to her side.

He bent down his head
         And gave her a kiss . . .
But she rose from her pillow
         And said, with a hiss . . .

'What are you doing!
         Get off me, you creep!
How dare you awake me
         From my beauty sleep!'

                    Jennifer Curry

The Doctor and the Clown

A sad man went to the doctor
Who took one look and guessed
That his visitor wasn't physically ill
But was certainly depressed.

'You're right, so right,' said the sad man,
'And I doubt if there's any cure
But I thought I should come to see you
Just to make doubly sure.'

'I'm glad that you did,' said the doctor
With a great big smile on his face,
'Because, as it just so happens,
You've come to the right place.

'I'm not going to give you a tonic
I'm not going to give you a pill
But I am going to give you a word of advice
And take it if you will.

'Last night I went to the circus
Which has just arrived in town
With a whole array of wonderful acts
But the best of them all is the clown.

'Grock is his name, and believe me
He's really a clown and a half.
He'll double you up in stitches
And remind you how to laugh.

50

'I can guarantee when you see him
Your troubles will melt away,
So book yourself a ringside seat
At once, without delay.'

The sad man thanked him, turned to go
And shuffled towards the door
While the doctor noticed that he looked
Even sadder than before.

51

'Take my word for it,' said the doctor,
'At least give the clown a chance.'
The sad man summoned a rueful smile
And looked at him askance.

Then it suddenly occurred to the doctor
To ask the patient's name.
'I know all about your problem
And the reason why you came

'But who exactly are you?'
The sad man bowed his head.
'Haven't you guessed already?
I am Grock,' he said.

John Mole

52

Lost

In a terrible fog I once lost my way,
Where I had wandered I could not say,
I found a signpost just by a fence,
But I could not read it, the fog was so dense.
Slowly but surely, frightened to roam,
I climbed up the post for my nearest way home,
Striking a match I turned cold and faint,
These were the words on it, 'Mind the wet paint.'

James Godden

I Come in Peace

The Alien stepped forwards,
It held its flippers high,
'I come in peace,' it whistled,
'From somewhere in the sky.'

The Earthling made no answer,
So the Alien tried again,
'Please take me to your leader –
I think my meaning's plain.'

No smiles disturbed the stillness
Of the Earthling's frosty face.
'Behold!' the Alien gurgled,
'I bring you gifts from Space.'

At last, when all its efforts
Had failed, and failed some more,
The Alien flew back homewards
To its friendly Alien shore.

But far away, its presents
Lay squashed between two cars,
While a rather puzzled petrol pump
Gazed blankly at the stars.

Clare Bevan

Careful With That,
You Might Break It

See what I've found.

Oh be careful with that,
It's so delicate, it could easily break.

If you take it in your hands gently,
you can hold it
close up to your eyes.

It's a bit hazy on the outside,
but if you wait for it to turn,
here and there you can see right through
and then you'll be really amazed!

Gently now, even though it looks solid enough,
you'd be surprised at just how flimsy it is.
Look there. Can you see the big blue bits?
I remember being so fascinated with them
that I wanted to touch them.

But you're not allowed to do that.
If you did, The High says you might damage it
because there's some protective coating
or gas or something surrounding the whole thing
and if that gets damaged, it could be serious.
What do you suppose the green bits are?

That's it, just let it rest in your palm.
Watch how it spins of its own accord.
Have you spotted the brown areas?
No, you mustn't touch the little white thing
going round it, The High says it's very important too,
a force or influence or balance perhaps.
Let's leave it now, careful, don't forget it's so very
    fragile.

It's name?
The High calls it Earth.
Some say it's a sad place.

                                John Rice

Phew!

Something's outside our tent
A slithery, snuffling noise
I don't know what it is
But I know that it eats boys.

Something's outside our tent
I bet it's big and hairy
With chomping jaws and bulging eyes
Looking very scary.

Something's outside our tent
It's grunting and it's near
Sounds like it could freeze my blood
Keep it out of here!

Something's outside our tent
I hope it's gone by morning.
Wait a tick, it's next door's tent
It's only Darren snoring!

David Harmer

Wilkins' Luck

Not liking work much, Wilkins looked instead
For bubble schemes to make his bread.
Heard of an island where resides
A peaceful people – all one-eyed.
Planned thus: sail there, seize a few;
These cyclopean freaks on view
Back home (at a stiff admission fee)
Would make his fortune easily.
Wilkins took ship and after many a while
Arrived at the green Pacific isle.
Discovered what he'd heard was true:
Each person had a single eye – and it was blue.
While Wilkins studied this strange feature,
'Look,' cried the islanders, 'a two-eyed creature!'
One smarter than the rest was heard to say,
'To see a freak like that . . . would people pay?'
Now Wilkins, caged, is twice a day on view
And wishes that he'd thought the matter through.

Eric Finney

59

An Inspector Calls

On the day before the visit
our teachers rushed round tidying the school.
Everyone helped. The youngest children
were sent to hunt along the skirting boards
and peer under low furniture, picking up
loose straw or feathers that the cleaning ladies
had missed and chasing out any hidden animals.
Mostly these were gerbils, though there was
a worrying business with a python in the paint
    cupboard.
The cats were cleared off the radiators and shooed
    outside
where they sat in a grumpy line along the playground
    wall.
Most of the reptiles were in tanks, which were
easily moved into the boiler room, though a few
    geckos
were still being brushed from walls late in the
    afternoon.

The parrots were a problem. Some of the older boys
wanted to spray them grey and put them outside
    disguised as pigeons,
but in the end some girls covered themselves in
    birdseed
and lured them down. After that it was easy to hide
    them in the toilets
where their noise would not be noticed. It took the
    combined force
of all the fourth-year classes, the headmaster and a
    mouse
to get the elephant into the janitor's room, but in the
    end

it was wedged between the shelves and buckets
and settled to eating hay and mops. It was decided
to disguise the monkeys as second-year boys – and indeed
you couldn't see much difference, except the monkeys were quieter.
Last of all, we herded the camels from the hall and tethered them
in the bike-shed. Only the fish tanks and caged mice were left
and when the inspector came next morning, the headmaster met him
with a confident smile.
Unfortunately, without the animals around,
the space and silence were irresistible holes to fill –
we started to riot, jumping and screaming, running and screeching.
The inspector stared, grim-faced. He said,
'It's like a zoo in here.'

Dave Calder

Chase

Tom knew it had begun.
He couldn't hear it.
He couldn't see it.
He couldn't feel it.

But it had started.
He could sense it,
Knew it was coming
After him.

The creature followed.
Huge, hairy
Fierce, ferocious
Grabbing, grasping.

Tom ran.
Blindly, boldly
Recklessly, randomly
Faster, furiously.

The creature continued.
Sniffing, searching
Peering, ploughing
Galloping, galumphing.

Tom dodged through forests.
Dark, dismal
Tangled, tortuous
Trashing, dashing.

Branches reached out.
Scratching, splintering
Weaving, waving.
Sharp, swaying.

Tom splashed through streams.
Bubbling, bursting
Slipping, splashing
Cascading, crashing.

Tired now.
Gasping, gulping
Groaning, moaning.
Wandering, wilting.

Tom began to climb.
Stepping, stumbling
Gripping, grabbing
Up and upwards.

The creature was closer.
He could hear it.
He could see it.
He could feel it.

It reached out for him.
Wizened, withered
Hard, hairy
Paw, claw.

It clutched at him.
'You're It!'
Turned and
raced
away.

L. A. Johnson

65

Sir Guy and the
Enchanted Princess

Through howling winds on a storm-tossed moor
Sir Guy came to a castle door.

He was led by some strange power
To the deepest dungeon of a ruined tower.

A princess sat on a jewelled throne
Her lovely features carved in stone.

His body trembled, was she dead?
Then her sweet voice filled his head.

'These evil spirits guard me well
Brave Sir Knight, please break their spell.

'Though I am stone, you shall see
Kiss me once, I shall be free.'

As demons howled she came to life
Blushed and whispered, 'Have you a wife?'

'My love,' he said, 'still remains
With collecting stamps and spotting trains

But as long as you do as you're told
I think you'll do, come on, it's cold.'

'Oh,' she cried, 'you weedy bore
I wish I was entranced once more.'

Lightning struck, the demons hissed
Sir Guy was stone, a voice croaked, 'Missed!'

The princess rode his horse away
And poor Sir Guy's still there today.

David Harmer

Aladdin Made Short

The cave was dark.
The cave was damp.
Aladdin rubbed
The rusty lamp.

Alas, the genie
Never came.
Wrong lamp.
What a shame.

(He's down there still,
I must report.
And so this version's
Very short.)

Kaye Umansky

The Last Shall Be First

Because I can't head a ball, nor even kick,
whenever we play soccer I am the last one picked.

Because I cannot bat or bowl or catch
I am the last one picked for the cricket match.

Because of all our class I am the one who is still small
I am the last one picked for the basketball.

I am the last one picked for rugby, cos I am not hard
    and tough.
I am the last one picked to play Tig, cos I am not fast
    enough.

In fact, whenever it comes to picking teams,
I am always the last one picked, it seems.

I am the last one picked for the choir, because I cannot
    sing.
I am the last one picked for everything.

Except when Miss asks a question I don't understand,
and nor does anyone else, so no one raises a hand,
so she looks round the class, and it makes me sick,
for that is the only time ever I am the first one picked.

McKee Warwick: Just Poets

From the Horse's Mouth

It was dusk as I strolled down a country lane
When a voice from nearby spoke plain as plain:

Did you know I won the Derby in seventy-three?
Yet when I turned round there was no one to see!

The fields stretched empty as the shadowy air
But for one old horse that was grazing there.

So on I walked down the darkening lane
When the same voice spoke, and said over again:

Did you know I won the Derby in seventy-three?
And when I looked, that horse was following me!

So I took to my heels, like a shot from a gun –
Three desperate miles to the Rising Sun.

I'd no breath to speak with as I fell through the door,
But they helped me as if they'd seen all this before.

'You've no need to explain,' the landlord said
As he drew me a pint, and shook his grey head.

'That old horse tells more lies than have ever been
        reckoned.
It was seventy-two, and the beast came second!'

Raymond Wilson

The Alien Sandwich Snatcher

An alien stole my sandwiches
When I was in the park,
He did it in broad daylight,
He didn't wait till dark.

He swooped across the climbing frame
With tentacles a-quiver,
He swiped my nice new lunch bag while
I paddled in the river.

He didn't stop to thank me,
He flew straight home to Space
With butter on his flippers
And a smile upon his face.

I hope the jam upsets him,
I hope he hates brown bread,
I hope he has the hiccups
In his little alien bed.

I hope he's feeling sorry
With my lunch bag in his beak,
And I hope my mum believes me –
It's the fifth I've lost this week.

Clare Bevan

Out of the Grey Silence

There's a monster in the fog:
I see its blurred shape loom
And lump along towards me
Out of the murk and gloom.
I'm alone in this grey silence
With its brown bulk coming on,
I'm rooted to the spot,
Much too terrified to run.
The grass stirs from its footsteps,
Scattering beads of dew,
I see its plumes of breath –
Then the creature utters:
'Moo!'

Eric Finney

73

Lost and Found

I was worrying over some homework
When my grandad walked into the room
And sat wearily down with a grunt and a frown
And a face full of sorrow and gloom.

'I've lost it, I've lost it,' he muttered,
'And it's very important to me.'
'Lost what?' I replied. 'I've forgotten,' he sighed.
'But it's something beginning with T.'

'A toffee, perhaps,' I suggested,
'Or a teapot or even your tie,
Or some toast or a thread . . .' but he shook his grey
    head
As a tear trickled out of one eye.

'A tuba,' I said, 'or some treacle,
Or a toggle to sew on your mac,
Or a tray or a ticket, a tree or a thicket,
A thistle, a taper, a tack.'

But Grandad looked blank. 'Well, some tweezers,
Or a theory,' I said, 'or a tooth,
Or a tap or a till or a thought or a thrill,
Or your trousers, a trestle, the truth.'

'It's none of these things,' grumbled Grandad.
'A toy trumpet,' I offered, 'a towel,
Or a trout, a tureen, an antique tambourine,
A toboggan, a tortoise, a trowel . . .'

Then suddenly Grandad's scowl vanished.
'I've remembered!' he cried with a shout.
'It's my temper, you brat, so come here and take that!'
And he boxed both my ears and went out.

Richard Edwards

I Just Don't Trust
the Furniture

I just don't trust the furniture
The desks have all got teeth
Grinning fangs inviting
Evilly delighting
At what they could be biting
And dragging down beneath . . .

Violet electric light
Bursts in violent blasts
Forked-tongue lightning slithers
Like vicious neon rivers
Everybody shivers
Until the storm has passed

No one knows just how or why
But when they start to glow
When open lids are gaping
There is no escaping
The scratching and the scraping
Of the horrors down below

A corridor is opened
A gateway is unfurled
Its gravity commences
To hypnotize the senses
And drag you down defenceless
To its nightmare world

I just don't trust the furniture
The dark decaying smell
But when hungry desks are humming
Their rumbling insides drumming
Something else is coming
Beware the chairs as well . . .

I just don't trust the furniture . . .

Paul Cookson

Barking

It wouldn't have been so awful,
it wouldn't have seemed so bad,
if the daft bloke in the spotlight
had been someone else's dad.

It wouldn't have been us embarrassed.
It wouldn't have been us who whinged.
Another family would have suffered.
Other relatives would have cringed.

But it was our dad up there.
It was our dad *having a go*.
It was our dad being laughed at.
Our dad was part of the show.

He said he wouldn't go under.
He claimed he could stay in control.
He would resist the hypnotist.
His will power we would extol.

But in no time Dad was barking
and crawling around on all fours.
He willingly begged for a biscuit
and whined to be let out of doors.

It really was a nightmare.
Not nice for his next of kin.
But when Dad returned to his seat
he swore he couldn't remember a thing.

Not acting like a Jack Russell?
Not being forced to sit up and beg?
'Not even,' he said, with a twinkle,
'biting that hypnotist's leg!'

Bernard Young

The Quest of the Red Prince
(A traditional Romany story)

'Please stay,' I said. I said, 'Don't go,'
As he cracked his stirrup leather.
But the Red Prince laughed with disgusted scorn
And threw me aside, like a coat outworn:
'My pledge is pledged and my oath is sworn!
I shall travel the world until I know
How to live forever!'

So the Red Prince rode and rode along
And his hoofs blazed sparks at night.
Rode round the world till he reached a wood
Whose trees like cathedral pillars stood,
Branches entwined: a brotherhood
Of rustling leaves and sweet birdsong
And dappling light.

'Tell me,' he called, called, 'Do you know
How to live till Eternity?'
Then the Red Prince listened, but all he heard
Were the monotone taps of a single bird,
Woodpecker pecking the same sole word
As it worked a hole like the O of No:
'Pit-tity, pit-ity, pity.'

So the horse ran on till she ran on sand
And salt spray soaked her red rider
And the Red Prince came face to face with the sea
Where the souls of the drowned float like ship's debris
And the shark and the whale keep company
And the seagulls squeal like a drunken band
And the sky is wider.

'Answer,' he yelled, yelled, 'Tell me, waves,
How I may live for evermore!'
But the rollers soughed and the combers sighed
And the dogged moon dragged and ragged the tide
And a sibilant voice hissed from deep inside
Trenches deeper than countless graves:
'On shore,' or perhaps, 'Unsure.'

So the Prince rode on till the dry earth cracked
Beneath the hoofs of his weary mare
And a desert as red as his red cloak lay –
All scorpion claws and wind-carved clay –
Frozen by night and scaled by day,
Its dunes rearing up their sharp-spined backs
Ferocious and bare.

He said to himself, 'This place must know –
This desert which never changes.'
But the soft sand shifted listlessly
And its pleated dunes smiled wistfully,
'Our mortal remains are all you see:
Alive we once stood crowned with snow:
We mountain ranges.'

For a million years he rode without rest,
Returning the way he had come;
Through a desert blown bare but for one last grain,
'Cross an ocean sipped dry but for one damp stain,
Past the woodpecker bones on a treeless plain,
And no one he'd met had solved his quest,
And his heart was numb.

'Welcome,' I said. I said, 'My door
All these years has waited, wide.'
And the Red Prince smiled at the welcome sight
Of a friendly face in the hollow night
I filled his eyes with my candle's light;
I answered all of his questions and more
And led him inside.

And I sang him an old familiar song,
I helped him catch his labouring breath;
And I bathed his eyes and I soothed his pain,
And over and over I spoke his name
While I promised he never need travel again,
For every journey, however long:
Ends in me . . . Death.

Geraldine McCaughrean

Invasion

Zigland the Great, Mighty Warlord of the planet Drob
Grand King and High Emperor of the Fifteen Galaxies
Dragon Slayer, Beast Killer, Destroyer of Monsters
landed firmly on the planet's surface, flourished
his Vorgle-blast Super-ray Gun that once smashed the
　　dreaded Smigz.
The Shield of Vambloot, which protected him from
　　harm
the Ring of Skigniblick, which gave him all power
and standing fast the mighty warrior
spoke out loudly, his voice ringing like the Great Bell
　　of Hootrim
I claim this planet and all its creatures for the Empire of
　　Drob
have great fear of me and my warriors, tremble at our
　　mighty voices.

Unfortunately
he was suddenly swallowed
by a passing magpie, who thought he was
a very juicy beetle.

David Harmer

83

Letters from Beauty
(Found in the post-dragon's lunch box)

Dear Daddy, I'm so lonely.
I'm living with a Beast –
It's true he owns a castle
Where EVERY meal's a feast,
But shadows in the mirror
Are full of gloom and sorrow . . .
PLEASE come and save your daughter
And take me home tomorrow.

Dear Dad, Perhaps my letter
Has somehow gone astray.
I'm STILL inside this palace,
I'm STILL locked up all day.
The Beast is creeping closer,
I hear him snort and roar . . .
Please take me home TOMORROW
(As I have asked before).

Dear Father, STILL no answer,
No sign of help at all.
The Beast is big and grumpy,
He prowls around the hall,
He growls around the garden,
He dribbles when he chews . . .
Please take me home THIS MINUTE,
Before I'm next week's news.

Dear Sir, It's been a fortnight
Since first I sent a note.
It's time you gave the answer
To all the things I wrote.
The Beast is keen on dancing,
He likes to twirl and bow,
He spins me round the ballroom . . .
Please take me home RIGHT NOW!

Dear Daddy, Scrap the rescue,
Don't try to set me free,
I kissed the Beast last Thursday
And we're happy as can be.
My fangs are sharp and spiky,
My fur is green and blue,
And Beasty seems quite handsome
Now I'm a monster too . . . xxxxx

Clare Bevan

A Cynical Man from Mauritius

A cynical man from Mauritius
Thought it foolish to be superstitious
When a black cat passed near
He stood firm, without fear
(What a shame that the panther was vicious).

Rachel Rooney

Index of Poets

Acknowledgements

The publishers wish to thank the following for permission to use copyright material:

Kaye Umansky, 'Aladdin Made Short' by permission of Oxford University Press; **Gerda Mayer**, 'The Crunch', first published in *The Candy-Floss Tree*, Oxford University Press 1984; **John Mole**, 'The Doctor and the Clown', first published in *The Wonder Dish*, Oxford University Press 2002; **Debjani Chatterjee**, 'Snake in School', first published in *Animal Antics*, Pennine Pens 2000; **Bernard Young**, 'Barking' and 'Moaning Minnie', first published by Hands Up Books 2004; Shel Silverstein, 'Batty', first published in *A Light in the Attic* copyright © Evil Eye Music, Inc., by permission of Edite Kroll Literary Agency Inc.

Every effort has been made to trace the copyright holders, but if any have been inadvertently overlooked the publishers will be pleased to make the necessary arrangement at the first opportnity.

A selected list of titles available from Macmillan Children's Books

The prices shown below are correct at the time of going to press. However, Macmillan Publishers reserves the right to show new retail prices on covers, which may differ from those previously advertised.

Surprising Joy		
A novel by Valerie Bloom	978-0-330-39860-2	£5.99
The Tribe		
A novel by Valerie Bloom	978-1-4050-4782-1	£9.99
There's a Hamster in the Fast Lane		
Poems chosen by Brian Moses	978-0-330-44423-1	£3.99
Taking Out the Tigers		
Poems by Brian Moses	978-0-330-41797-6	£3.99

All Pan Macmillan titles can be ordered from our website, www.panmacmillan.com, or from your local bookshop and are also available by post from:

**Bookpost,
PO Box 29, Douglas, Isle of Man IM99 1BQ**

Credit cards accepted. For details:
Telephone: 01624 677237
Fax: 01624 670923
Email: bookshop@enterprise.net
www.bookpost.co.uk

Free postage and packing in the United Kingdom